SUSPENSION BRIDGE

By ROD MCKUEN

BOOKS

Poetry

And Autumn Came
Stanyan Street & Other
   Sorrows
Listen to the Warm
Lonesome Cities
In Someone's Shadow
Caught in the Quiet
Fields of Wonder
And to Each Season
Come to Me in Silence
Moment to Moment
Celebrations of the Heart
Beyond the Boardwalk
The Sea Around Me
Coming Close to the Earth
We Touch the Sky
The Power Bright & Shining
The Beautiful Strangers
The Sound of Solitude
Suspension Bridge

The Rod McKuen Omnibus
Hand in Hand
Love's Been Good to Me
Looking For a Friend
Too Many Midnights
Watch for the Wind

Prose

Finding My Father
An Outstretched Hand

Et Cetera

A Book of Days
A Book of Days, Vol. 2
Another Beautiful Day

Music Collections

New Carols for Christmas
The McKuen/Sinatra
   Songbook
New Ballads
At Carnegie Hall
28 Greatest Hits
Through European
   Windows
The Songs of Rod McKuen,
   Vol. 1
The Songs of Rod McKuen,
   Vol. 2

Collected Poems

Twelve Years of Christmas
A Man Alone
With Love . . .
The Carols of Christmas
Seasons in the Sun
Alone

MUSIC

Concertos

For Piano & Orchestra
For Cello & Orchestra
For Guitar & Orchestra
#2 for Piano & Orchestra
For Four Harpsichords
Seascapes for Piano
The Woodwinds

Symphonies, Symphonic Suites, etc.

Symphony No. 1
Ballad of Distances
The City
4 Quartets for Piano & Strings
4 Trios for Piano & Strings
Adagio for Harp & Strings
Rigadoon for Orchestra
Pastures Green/ Pavements Gray
Piano Quartets
String Quartets
Symphony No. 4

Ballet

Americana, R.F.D.

Point/Counterpoint
Elizabethan Dances
The Minotaur (Man to Himself)
Volga Song
Full Circle
The Plains of My Country
The Man Who Tracked the Stars
Birch Trees
Liberty
I'm Not Afraid (with Jacques Brel)
Seven Cynical Songs

Major Film Scores

The Prime of Miss Jean Brodie
A Boy Named Charlie Brown
Joanna
The Unknown War
Scandalous John
The Borrowers
Lisa Bright & Dark
Emily
Travels with Charley
The Beach

CHEVAL BOOKS   HARPER & ROW, PUBLISHERS

Los Angeles   New York
New York   Cambridge, Philadelphia
Sydney   San Francisco, London
Johannesburg   Mexico City, São Paulo
London   Singapore, Sydney

Rod McKuen

SUSPENSION BRIDGE

SUSPENSION BRIDGE. Copyright © 1984 by Rod McKuen and
Montcalm Productions, Inc. All rights reserved. Printed in the
United States of America. No part of this book may be used or
reproduced in any manner whatsoever without written
permission except in the case of brief quotations embodied in
critical articles and reviews. For information address Harper &
Row, Publishers, Inc., 10 East 53rd Street, New York, N.Y.
10022. Published simultaneously in Canada by Fitzhenry &
Whiteside Limited, Toronto.

FIRST EDITION

Designed by Ruth Bornschlegel

Library of Congress Cataloging in Publication Data

McKuen, Rod.
  Suspension bridge.

  Includes index.
  I. Title.
PS3525.A264S85   1984   811'.54   84-47589
ISBN 0-06-015348-2 (Harper & Row)

84 85 86 87 88 10 9 8 7 6 5 4 3 2 1

Au suivant

Contents

Bridges

Some seasons stall or do not come. They dawdle past agreed appointments becoming useless to the nature need and thus unnecessary hooks for memory. Spring stays spring so long it passes summer in a lazy relay, becoming fall or one more page of spring.

New Year's Day will oft-times entreat the summer to arrive—the man who came to dinner stays and fills the first six months of given year with sunlight hard enough to make each twig a Diamond safety match awaiting tinder-brush and hard rock August flint.

Who forgets the winter out of season, gone mad inside America's middle? Flood and twister, fist hailstones in Denver June, Oklahoma redesigned as lake, Montana ten months digging out in hopes commencement exercises can be held on light green field . . . New York with alternate complaints of Frigidaire and turned-up microwave. California one year haywire from a winter insurance carrier's blot from memory, followed by a drought confounding television weather personalities.

For me, the fall, however ill or well it comes, is paramount. I relive/re-enhance first romances, glory in blue blossom trees that never fail. Ever I entreat the white azaleas in the back garden to blossom, dry and bloom again. I am at home in autumn, rain and dour countenance accepted. Autumn is the time when seasons merge because of bare necessity. It is a time of coming to and going from real reality.

Every poem out of me, choosing poem cycle then stacking high enough to be a book, has square root in seasons. Nature is not the always arbiter—there are those seasons of the heart, the groin, dreamed vacation, and that damp day not coming often when the mind and tongue decide to merge.

One season is guised in nature and titled *Winter in America*. The other chapters are soul seasons and less structured. They are the hard parts: the meat in them remains inside the bones. Yet like the quartered year each is a bridge to neighbor.

I have come across my country again in all four seasons. I found it to be healthy enough . . . its people resourceful, big friends in good humor. We are all of us working toward the same ends.

R.M./June 1984

Author's Note

Some of these poems first appeared in *Folio*, the quarterly journal of poetry. "The Best Embraces" and "Nebraska Sonnets" are from works in progress. "Christchurch to Duneden" was written in 1982 in New Zealand. The remaining poems were written in 1983/84 in Southern California. The title *Winter in America* is taken from the song of the same name written by Australian composer Doug Ashdown.

SUSPENSION BRIDGE

Winter in America

for Rose Adkins

Hardware in a life is unavoidable
but it's the softer stuff
           that makes a life.
And thus we come to winter.
It is not the iceberg we remember.
The snowflake only.

Winter in America

Smoke winds in columns ever up
unending furnace, appetite unquenched
              and it will snow forever.
The cries of birds misjudging seasons
ring like bobsled bells, hill to valley
eave of barn to kitchen doorway.
The kitchen cat stops milk-drunk
                          near the sink.
Unspools herself, spools up again and sleeps.
Everything is fading.
The sky, the ground, the earth frame.
                          Everything.

And love
so small a thing to loom so big
              in every snowman's life
is lost or gone away again. To spring perhaps.

Come home milkmaid, from the milking shed.

Mirrors everywhere, look there in ice
your own face frowning back,
another year and still no wise men
              coming from the East.

Another year
where every sunset caught is forfeit
given back to its horizon line.
Winter will be long again,
                    winter will be long.
The cowherd boys are grumbling
and pickups take an hour to start.
We've lost the heart of everything
                    to slush.

In the street outside of town
no dogs raise their heads to bark.

The snow's lieutenant, sleet,
begins a walking of the guard.
Beyond the window and beyond
the fields are frozen frescos,
                    picture cards.
Not beautiful, but flawed
as though a crazed mechanic
worked too long,
            too hard on it—
a spotless, gleaming engine
that will not run.

The lord's off dozing, with the cattle
                        or the lord of manor
and doesn't care.
And yet to see it is to know
that so much love
has gone into this country's
                        countryscape,
as if the whole United States
has been reshaped
to fit a smaller definition.
My country, my America,
you are the frozen north
at north and south and in-between.
You're mean as age and getting meaner.
Were I God
I'd be ashamed
to show my face in such a clime.
Coast to coast it's wintertime.
Even stars have snowy coverlets.

Lillian at Fifty

Snow has now begun to comb her hair,
soft patch of winter at each temple
where only summer grew before.
Her voice thick-throated,
a murmured whisper in the pines.
And there are lines
            about the corners of her eyes
more beautiful than love words written down
and sent away, Browning to Browning.
Her breasts no longer point immodestly—
they bend and curve
and fit into her body curve,
the way a lover's arm was meant
to cradle that so-perfect head just found.

From bath to bedroom and to bed.

She is not just that perfect woman
                            in my life
but premier woman of the world,
created wholly by herself,
made up to make a mold for womanhood.
And I, mortal lover of immortality,
what man could dream up heaven better
than she who lets the snow begin
                    to softly comb her hair?

River House

Fish hawks fly above the reeds
and locomotives still pass on
catching in their throats
the dust of one more year
and belching it again into the air.
I go a-berrying for wax gooseberries
to rape the moon-raked fields
                      of aborigines
long dead and underground,
only black flints left for tracings.
The country keeps erasing its own heritage.

I war with dragonfly and worker ant
                    for my own share
of nature's dropped obscurities.
Albino butterfly on branch,
a speckled roach inside woodpecker drillings.

The columns off at River House
are white, spit polish, shining.
Beyond them rolls the Hudson on and on
and farther still more trees, more reed—
Spring jungle for the house cats,
out after field mouse,
                            wounded sparrow.
Don't they know it's winter?
Quail and woodchuck mix it up
            and neither is the winner.
I've tried to catch it all
            inside a Polaroid
but all I get are blues,
unheard-of reds and yellow hues.

The weekend guests are late again
and I've been up at eight again.

Black birch here and lilac soon
bats and starlings duel at sunset
dive bombers in a certain death
then pulling back a foot from ground.

The queen ant's had a castle
                built around her—
drones, workers, cousin bees bring twigs
and sand grains for the monument.
Even River House has yet to see
                so many guests.
Serenity lives in these acres.
I could watch the anthill all day long.
Another cat. How many are here quartered?
Mice have to feel this place a no-mouse land.

A fox is stealing chickens
in some ramshackle chicken shack,
you hear mad cackling at different hours.
A hare is in the middle distance,
                         ears straight up.
The final pumpkin falls
from worn-out withered vine
and frost police descend from branch
                         and bough.
Walter, bring the groceries in
the other guests have come.

Genesis Revisited

Here is some grand arrangement,
some complicated and divine mosaic.
Look between a child's downy hair
and that chin-chin forming
and you will find eyes deeper than
                            the soul is deep,
and floating on the tops of them
unstructured, unformed thoughts
part of past and coming generations.

Civilizations, civilizations
alliterations of those things
that only float in children's eyes.

The size of skies is not intimidating
                            to a child
not energy or atom can compete
with that subculture nourished,
then brought forward from the womb.

With each new child
we go from strength to strength.
Umbilical, as always, saves us.
To those who fear
the future colorless as eiderdown
                    against the snow
I say contrast, even white on white
comes up against itself most vividly.

As soot is softer
than the coal it comes from
so too is pollen different than the mother stem.
Our differences will always give us sameness,
continuation through the decades.

Child, child, you are the promise
new bud bursting into pretty petal
as long as we have you,
your daughters and your sons upcoming,
we are of independent means.

Over at Our House

My Papa's gone to Michigan
my brother's in the slammer
Emma's serving fish again,
                                    damn her.

My old maid aunt
would rave and rant
and talk of the Depression
and lock herself inside her room
when Congress was in session.

Brother Bill went down the hill
to fetch the Nouveau Beaujolais
Sister swallowed all his guppies,
                                    spanked the puppies,
and chased the cat away.

The boys are playing kick-the-can
the girls are jumping rope
I wish that I were Charlie Chan,
Mickey Mouse or Pope.

Last Refuge

Eternity will leave us soon enough
            returning to eternity
and we will have our old trees
back again and green.
The flowers
of that now far-distant spring
will come at us on chargers
            at full gallop.
That single promise keeps
the frost outside the heart.
Here where all is frozen over,
taken in the January glass
that cracks and falls to pieces,
we see every bird that stops to rest
                        on icy branch
as omen.

Holly from Above

for Dean Ekdahl

A capital view of holly trees
green laurel and the plum
as we glide low and nearly slam a fence.
Holly from the top is scarecrowlike
all jagged edges reaching out
                to paw the air.
Such a prickly Christmas stuff
with not the symmetry of evergreen
or stately stationary pine,
it is as if a vine pushed on its own
away from fence or trellis
and went seeking clouds
only to be toed down flat
              by heaven's foot.

Laurel is laurel, I'll give it that
        and plum proud plum
but none could see
a holly tree from up above
and honor it with carols.

This dwarf not even good enough
for larger trees to squat upon
is barbed wire sure as metal
        intertwined with spikes,
the likes of it no different from
tacks scattered to ensnare
        the nighttime bandit.

Rest on, you gentlemen too merry
to observe the upper half
        of holly branch
before you placed it on the altar
        of a mass for Christ.

Some beauty stops
on anything dark green in color,
but holly should have been
            Good Friday flower,
a wreath of it a simile
            for crown of thorns
with berries to remind us of the blood
that dripped from off His head
to shoulder, then to ground.

Holly seen from eighty-foot balloon
                            descending,
it stands out as material
to top off crucifixions.

America

A wondrous thing it is to have
    a country you can love,
a field to lie with,
hill to hike,
a patch of woods so honorable
it stands as its own creed.
Cities too within the land
that belch and puff and bubble up
mixing native/foreign colors
            of its people,
each contributing.

It is a healthy wondrous thing
to have a country you can love.

The Truthful Lover

Only out of small things
  does the whole come.

The Truthful Lover

for Chen Sam

How fragile are the dreams
          that cross and meet
and make up love.
As need is but a plain name for desire
so too the lies that lovers use in conquest
should be held to light,
cost and consequence not pushed aside.
Whenever love comes calling in the night
              truth bends a little.
That is to be expected.
Love is a non-exclusive instrument.
It is a savings bank,
interest computed and compounded
high above the principal.
It is a place to gather
where lover and beloved
            never come as equals.
And yet the body at its widest
is no wider than the brain that drives it.

Who is the truthful lover,
                    how can we know?
Supposing we pass over that *one*
who seems like all the rest,
            but only comes by once?
In doing so we forfeit life
and its best feature, laughter.

How is Aphrodite now and where is she?
And if she called us each by name
would we discern her voice
in crowded room or reverie?
The questions pile.
The answers run down through the distance
                like a world unwinding.

In love there is no training ground,
only happy accidents.

Sacrament

I like my body lying next to yours.

My leg against your leg and over it
the muscle quivering to touch
the luxury of thighs that open onto thighs.
I like our sighs together and I like
my body lying next to yours at night
                    and every morning.

I wear you
coming next to you
as I would clean cotton shirt
soft to the touch you are and tingling.
And everything you touch
is but a punctuation to yourself.

I love the loss of vagrancy inside your arms
your fingers swarming on my back
              like bees attacking single flower.
The light from out your eyelids coming.
The puzzled humming in my ear
as you nod yes not having heard
the question that I asked.
Your hair unmasked for what it is—
a tangled web of craziness
is like a whim not taken up.
So too your mouth is glowing, fair,
runs hot and cold and in no pattern.
I like our elbows, noses, knees
interrupting rhythms that should be truer.
Your breasts are skillful, genius each,
priceless in a bed world
whose currency is chance.

I love the ample of you
                  and the lean
the part of you expecting flesh
and rising up to meet it.

The symmetry of you is what I love
                  odd angles too
those energy propelling sighs
and little cries from you.
The ivory underside of you
the tanned and glowing legs and arms.

I love the wind of you
as much as the unwinding.
The kindness of your inner ear
is more than I can bear to speak about.

All honey to the heart,
all pasture to the eyes
the size of you is one great breath
taken in, held, not expelled, not ever.
Ingenious are your ankles, calves, hips
stepping stones to that great wonder
                              on ahead.

What I love most in all the world
is my own body next to yours.
It is a vanity, a wonderful conceit.

Galileo's Toolbox

I cannot measure you by height
nor depth discerned by meter, mile.
The breadth of your thought and its frame
cannot be charged against
what ordinary wides are.

By your side
my own size shrinks
and yet you swell my every heart.
You are the whole of everything,
world smashing into world,
sun spinning in your upper frame.
The yardstick and the tape unspooled
do not suffice as instruments
                    to check your size.

Either/Or

Since you have known me
                all my life
I would that I could be aboard
the final ship you sail
to see you out of yours.
Yet I could never think up life
        in form or substance,
ill health or well, without you.
What then to be preferred,
me catching you before God
                in His heaven does
or you behind
to sort my papers out
as I slip silently from sight.

Death ought to take us both at once
but who'd be left to sweep
the worn-out flesh away,
to put it in its proper mound.
Who'd be around to tidy up?

Careless is the plan of nature,
timetable of the lesser things
                              like man.
We are invented and thought up
but have so little say
in how we come or go
and come again if we do come.

In truth while immortality
                  is each man's goal
I'd rather be the first to go—
if all my needs could be administered
                  by one who cares.
Should lightning strike
I know you'd run and sweep
                  the ashes up
to keep the litter from encroaching on
                  the right of way of others.

A Promise

When all the trees have been dismantled
the decorations of their leaves set by
                    birch to brown, maple to black
roots pulled up and tumbled in a pile
and when the sun has scurried
up from darkness and back to darkness
                    for the final time,
with every ocean gone
leaving only traces, a ring around its rim,
then I will love you more than now.

We will have gone beyond impossibles
            with no restraining rein
and we will both come back again
to this same place.
I will love you better then and more.
I will have learned from loving
                    how to love.

Future and the Past Defined by Grief

Grief in its passing
leaves but little light.
The night sky mantle
          with a single star,
the roadside just across the street,
blurred like the hedge grown wild
without the trimmer's shears.
It has a solitary patch of white
a preview of a thing upcoming,
the echo of a thing long past.
It swells itself to resignation,
moves to bitterness then grief again
till even changing season
                    and thus opportunity
cannot uncloud the misted brain,
move awkward mantle off from tired heart.

Why carry yesterday toward tomorrow?
You only drag down forward hiker
and snare the winner in her stride.
Future and the past defined by grief
kill memory and rob imagination too.
There are too many thieves about.
Why add another rogue
to overcrowded gallery?

Kanon & Adagio

Too soon
the lovers fall from grace
and beds of their own making.
Not grace from heaven,
                        but themselves,
each the same steamboat that paddles
down life's most reckless rapids.

Beds of love are ever
beds of mistrust and of danger.
We always set upon and rob each other
of that most precious gift, ourselves.

Love wears the rainbow
                        on its cheek
as sure as any high sky does
and yet dark colors of the spectrum
            come with frequency and speed.

Not even flashing warning sign
can stop the lemming lover
from his leap into the darkness.
And yet, and yet
the counter melody of hope
rides with him past the cliff
                        and down.

Abandon Song

One day when you've abandoned me,
gone off with ferry man or tally man,
joined the circus, wooed the athlete
    from his training camp
and with your lover
crawled along blue highways out of sight,
then I will go a-running
toward the Maypole
    and the gypsy camp.
Seaward, always seaward,
pretending you back in my life.
I'll be the glad adventurer,
intrepid drummer in a band
that earns its way to orchestra.

I'll hide in music
or anyway in music stands
and when you come
on hands and knees
        in search of me
you'll have to wait till intermission
or when all the second violins
                are packed.
That is, if you come back.

Suspension Bridge

for David Long

A line strung canyon wall
       to canyon wall
will bring the canyon close enough
to bridge some empty air.
Far from danger you will find
a hint of friendship lurking,
even in the pilings.

Suspension Bridge

What mystery do you suppose
singes sky when daybreak comes?
Is it some crimson coil unspun
unraveled from the corners
of onlookers' eyes
or merely one great yawn,
a waking up of some behemoth
pink tongue flicking from
a deeper, darker throat?

Stand bareheaded on the sidewalk, shore
and feel saliva mist roll forward
around, around and over you—
retreat it will and come again
wave over wave in A.M. hour.

Magicians and mythology
could not work out
the sense of *other*
the sureness that *Beyond*
is where we live in now,
each of us
              a changeling
when the night erupts.
It is then the odd thought travels
                    with immunity.

Sweet, scary and delectable ideas
empower midnight hour
and the six that follow.
Thought that would not brave
                    the daylight
is brazen hussy after dark.

Acadia and Salem may make
convenants with spirit life
but they are not exclusive contracts.
It's not a witch's brew, I tell you
nothing warlock-like,
and no evil hinted at.
It's only *something*,
a concentrate let loose
              that runs amok.
You would not know it
if it came reflected up at you
              from private basin.
All the same,
It is a welcome gift.
Be grateful for the gift that comes
without instruction or condition—
except, perhaps, to feel.

Open Invitation

for Sister Mark Sandy

We will go and find the outer banks
comparing love to turning year,
give thanks to what the seasons say
not what we think we hear.

I know the roadway to those towns
the mind imagines or puts off.
It lies a little way beyond the cities
hands, not hearts, have formed.
And you may join me if you like,
all travelers were meant to have
fellow journeyman and good companion—
another who believes that buried treasure
lies on every riverbank or hill.
Someone bringing spade and map
and inspiration tucked beneath an arm
that's always open to the moment.

Heartland

for Andrew Praschak

The ditch between experience
                    and innocence
is not so wide.
Each has its outer edges
and its other side.

The sound that works to resonance
                    and later echo
must have that first initial strike.
And what of oceans,
                    tide and tidal,
that first vital sign a trickle
                    or a stream
must start the motion.

Experience is only an exaggeration
                    of that first dent in innocence.
We know the milky way
and Edison strung out his stars
but still we go in quest of fire.

Waiting It Out

Who hears the lone bark
                of the dog
without a master or a hearth,
the cat cry in the shadow
of the unattended house,
the moans of lovers when they learn
courage is not quite enough.
Who listens? Not the wind.
And sometimes even God is deaf
                    to the abandoned.

Be not afraid.
Life is not measured by the give and take,
the yardstick's only life itself.

Single

Ah, the sense of altogetherness
that single brings.
It is not unlike the rat-a-tat
        of rain artillery
that makes a puddle
then a lake.
Done right it dignifies a life.

Single in all things. Outsider.
Masked bandit on the run.
"There goes the territory,"
                couples shout.
I think it is a cry of envy
from those who traded freedom
for what they hoped was sensibility.

Some trade up again—
            not the same.
Once inside you cannot be an outlaw.
First grade is not taught
without a certain innocence.
Plateau number one
is the only starting point.
Single. One word.
And that is all it is, one word,
solo and not magnified.

Life—As Opposed to Time

Cities should be built
at either end
of every highway;
so that leaving somewhere
you are always going somewhere.

In taking the cloth
it's not the abstinence that kills
but all those wafers on the tongue—
so too the lack of going nowhere
          is not the problem.
It's the lack of having no one
to go there with.

Paraphrase

for Roberto Muñoz

When they come for me
        let them in.
Don't worry the door
by barring it.
To what end nostalgia?
Only the room advances.
Only our days come forward
to praise our other days.

I could dye my muscles
as a first disguise but always
I would want to swim.
When they come for me,
let them in.

We conquer our days daily.
Surprise each sunrise as it arrives.
The dream is always developing.
It never comes complete.
We are victim of intrepidation,
                    not tradition.
However heroic beads may be
unless you really believe
the rosary's only another string.
Infinity owes me something still,
so when they come for me
                    let them in.

The Runner from the Summer Games

The summer's done
and we are blessed
in turn by Mars and Mercury.
One warring while the other flees
and here comes Emma Goldman
                    with a stopwatch.

Retreating armies
never knew these paths
whose gates were closed to all
                    but running scoundrels.
Those left behind to make the body count
joined the body count.
The few who went ahead were carried,
                    not on shoulders but by hope.

But what is all of this
to gladiators of another time?
Fat rumor and tall story told
                    retold.
If there's to be another
                    Great Crusade
it ought to be bipartisan
                    and soon.
You bear the musket, shield the sword
I'll sell *Watchtower* and *Awake,*
and I will be there waiting on the dock
to welcome you aboard the frigate,
shelled and sinking to Atlantis.

God grant us kind contrition
for our sins and our omissions.
And most of all our contradictions.

One war blurs into another war.
Some peace exists for planting
                    next year's seed.
And with the lateness of the hour
power is another lump of something,
cold, uninteresting and not invited in.

Where is Homer when we need him?
Pounding the beat
of some far distant city block,
bending a board that helps to make an ark,
ring around the roseying in the park.

Do you propose a rose on every flag,
or have we all cried
Je suis fort mais j'aime la rose
                    too often?

The View from Houma Boulevard

Did you win or lose in Iowa,
did wine go dribbling
                down your chin
after the game and on the airplane home?
I'm sorry cold comfort in a letter
was all that waited as a welcome
when you came back to bayou country.

Long are the days in Louisiana,
                longer the nights.
Shallow the graves where water rises
old bones gray just out of sight.
For us the living there should be more
                than shadows of hanging moss.

Win or lose, apart is a loss.

Football

It is because of my own inability
to discern messages on time
that I send words into the air
straight, though, never at random.
Paper airplane hopes unleashed
                    in unsuspecting lands
made by hands that would have made
                              a difference
if they knew how.

For those same reasons
I'm confetti spreader at the Mardi Gras,
wherever saints or non-saints march.
Here too my handfuls are directional.

I believe that to each David
should come his Michelangelo
or why is marble dredged from quarry?
To each Eliza, her Bernard
or how is language guarded?
Without a caring Carroll
                    for each Alice,
Black Holes would pock the landscape.
Those of us who've chosen servitude
and put on uniforms to prove it
ought to keep antennas out.

The long and short of it,
to each David his own Michelangelo.
It justifies the uncarved stone.

Wait, and You Will See the Night Sky

Dawn is coming like the shepherd does
as silent as the sheep cry and as soon.
Voices rise from every *métairie*—
in time they'll form a choir and call it noon.
Dusk then at day's end. Night free.

Let every song that would be sung, be sung
once only or forever if there's cause.
Night never meant its walkers any harm,
go gently then and know that you belong.

If there is something not yet understood
let's bring it to the foreground and be done.
Only out of openness come answers,
vanishing as quickly as they come—
each making way for would not to be would.

Years from now you'll not remember why,
only that it happened and on time
underneath protective touch and arm.

In life, through stars,
don't look for easy climb.
Open out your hand and have a try.

I know the soul is always outward bound
not nestled in a safe place for too long.
Each body is but harbor for a time,
each harbor's depth is measured by its sound.

Do not believe the old dividing line.
You will find your own line soon enough.
Out of darkness, further darkness
unlike the dark behind.

Never fear the night sky,
only clocks unwind.
Who comes forward to define meantime?

Backpacking

I stepped down from the train near dawn.
A small wind blew across the tracks
                and toward the station house
then back again to hit my face whip-like.
A warning to remind the stranger
he would always be The Stranger.

This was not to be my Xanadu
where lost horizons swell and meet
and age and anonymity are sweet as sunrise.
My Land o' Lakes the size of skies,
my butterfly-filled canyon not so new
but mine no less than if I'd dug it with
                my hand as spade.

Another place to travel to
                then quickly from.
Not even time to fiddle with my backpack
                or adjust my smile.
Hidden sentinels are worst of all,
the ones who say, "be gone"
and give no reason for the banishment.

I did have time to see some rainbow droppings
slightly north of graying depot
                    and the sidecar sidings.
Many-colored and odd-angled,
slices of some larger framework broken up
still shining, though, and perfect
                    in their imperfection.
A curiosity unrevealed.

Perhaps like missile silos I had seen
                    outside of Moscow once
and later on, their cousins in Nebraskaland—
                    near my own farm—
these chunks of color were off-limits
to the interloper.

Shifty eyes will tell
                    and I was looking
but not for secrets in a landscape.
Only those the stranger celebrates
                    with other stranger.

The engine now was speaking up impatiently.

Before the warning whistle blew a second time
I turned and without looking back again
climbed aboard the same train
                    that had brought me here
and would take me further on.
Ever new beginnings or new endings.
Is there a difference?

Such memories I have,
some evenings later sitting here,
all jarred and sealed and put away,
(like peach preserves or berry jam)
of that far town I traveled to.
Minute memories, rim reflections
of what I did not get to know
                    but knew.

Some journeys are not trips at all
but larger journeys all the same
they define finite and give a name to need.
                              But they disturb.
If it were left to science
every new discovery would be made
to march into the square blindfolded.
Not so that it could not see daylight
but so that we might never see its eyes.

Roses

The river is cream foam
          churned up by tugs
that spit and sputter through her
slowly like an early thaw.
And there amid the agonies
that curse the stars,
on far banks, rows of roses.

Something only native to my blood
          is running 'round me
like an unrhymed rime.
I am in awe of having come
          this far
without a turning.

The odor of the roses now
is all that's left of roses.
I greet the morning head erect
the way a rose turns up
          toward sun's invitation.
And when the odor of the rose
is all that's left of roses
I will learn to love the beauty
          of the stem.

My buffalo will find me soon enough,
for now I play in blockhouse towns
of my own building.

Some messages are not received,
                 some never sent.
Some errands are not undertaken
as there are horses still at post.

And all that's left of roses
             is the smell of roses
and roses are what I'll miss most.

Back to San Francisco

You lie bent up in embryo sleep
below the painting of the blue fisherman
                without a pillow.
The checkered cover kicked and tangled on the
    floor
the old house creaking now
a car going by
the wind
a fire engine up the hill.

from *Stanyan Street & Other Sorrows*, 1966

It Is the Time of Year

The mountains come and go at liberty
inside, outside constant fog
that tugs each wave to shore
then slowly pushes it away.
Sea and fog in solid rhythm
with no room for lap or overlap.
When stray wave nibbles at a rock
the fog moves in to chase it
back into unbroken line.

It is the time of year
when waves rebuild
the beaches they destroyed
some seasons back,
when gulls move inland
for midweek trips—
thrift vacations near spring water.

The calligraphy of swallows
captions every sunset.
Bells ring somewhere, stealing sunlight,
                    hoarding sky.

I climb a higher cliff
to watch the silhouettes
going to the water,
                    coming from the water.
Now moonlight in flat waterfall
a path that widens, yellow, gold.
And certain birds at certain times
come winging through a hole of mist
and overhead toward a hill
that wasn't there an hour ago
and will be gone an hour from now.

Some reveries are interrupted
by other serenades.
A thought of spring
will somehow bring a summer back.
A certain face dissolves to favorite cat
                    in perfect sleep,
and there are solitudes unbroken
as there are reveries as yet untapped.
If we could tag each something else
it wouldn't be a something else.
Mystery is all there is to mystery
unless you count the coming on of it.

I am mapping out the scene before me,
                    with great care
storing it in overcrowded back head cell.
If I am ever dead to dreaming
I can one day call upon
an early summer afternoon dissolving
                    into a perfect summer night.
A time when swimmers,
sunlight still alight on each one's chest,
stayed unafraid to meet the dark,
seeking out that never-never place between
the valley and the mountain.

The Voice of Independent Means

Stars,
if I could read you then I would.
Life goes on forever,
Youth lasts an hour, maybe less.
As the gangplank comes in nearer
I speed away behind an engine
warming up, left running.
Could I erase the deficit
            and start again
I would not.
The beast too listens in the dark
for words that will not come,
is frightened by the stars
            and goes off running
like the rest of us.

All out there, stars and signposts
        voices too in twos and threes,
I know you are not enemies,
                but friends
not yet so labeled
        and collected.

Twilight passes like the tide
        all hushed and strange.
We only see time's changes
when it is late and growing later.
Gabriel does not rejoice
                at each new crowd
he only waits.

Oh lover, singing
                out beyond the wood
do not bruise me with false cries.
                Lullabies, lullabies,
sing me only lullabies.
Yours is the only song
that soars above the rest
and yours the only voice
of independent means.

Stars I'd reach and pick you
                if I could
and ancient, newer loves
                I'd do the same.

We'll all go home when winter comes
for now the seasons will not change
they are a shawl of ribbons, paper, rags
a willow dragging branches in the water.
Those voices and that voice
still singing in the not so wilderness,
still offering a song so sweet
that all the stars now take it up
and pass it down and on to us.

Comes the Colors

We prop old dreams against the wall
colors of the new-found day and night
                              our lexicon.
To each his own sweet tongue, I know,
but let our budding language be
not one of shadows but of shades and hues
drawn from that great roulette, rainbow wheel.

Armed with vivids, not with grays
we will hunt, track down and bring the old
                              to new reality.
Apollo has no lesser temple than shy Venus,
only different highways lead us
                              to her hideaway.
As war is but a breath away from peace
so too contentment is the last door entered.

What colors.
What stately and barbaric hues
the unexpected summer in midwinter brings.
It is the night wind once more pianissimo
soft-pedaling its wares.
What splendid cloth, what merchandise,
kaleidoscopic sunsets twice around.

Go gingerly.
Or better still, come go with me.
Ours ears have always heard like music.

Lower Montgomery Street

A bulldog
saunters down the white dividing line
no less menacing with tail awag,
he brags about his ugly beauty
                                    every step.
Behind him two boys throw a ball
forth and back, forth and back
reaching up and bending
boy children in a nonatomic catch.

A hill still farther back
comes coasting from a higher hill.
There is no high drive
on this too warm summer/winter day,
only deft, low gear meanderings.

Random motion.
A ball midair, two young men,
slow overhand, slower underhand.
A bulldog at the corner, Churchill.
A tall black lady, fashion's captive,
is passing, passes, passes on
the smell of mingled blossoms
                    lingers in her wake.
There is no mistaking costly scent,
like beauty it is not approximated.

The boys come closer
with their silver sphere
its oval arch is ever higher.
Above pedestrians it sails a little
until they stretch to bring it down.
A woman passes with an unformed frown,
too many boxes carried in her arms.

And on that same slow coasting hill
a row of pastel houses or façades
sits quiet as premeditation.
A little car is at the corner,
                    undecided.
South toward the docks,
east to meet Embarcadero,
up the hill again and over? What?
Joggers crisscross in a thought-out pattern.
The heart is stopped
by one young girl not yet aware
of her capacity to still the heart.
And suddenly there is no suddenly
as nothing happens that will make
the broadsheet, evening news.

On and on, continuing
two young men, once boys
when they were further down the block,
send a tired football through the air.
A secret sexercise for those
who only watch and want.

Life moves and moves
without a hint of interruption.
But little dreams and lesser dramas
each different and the same
are acted, played out hourly
                on Montgomery Street,
the lower end down near the bay.

Coming back to San Francisco
is not unlike reopening
        an envelope unopened—
You know that you will be amazed
and dazzled by its content,
but just how dazzling
the prize inside turns out to be
        is still beyond
the credibility of eye and heart.

The Stanyan Cafe

I always knew the old cafe
was made up just for us,
why else were our own memories
its only yellow pages?
I heard somewhere or thought I heard
                    that it closed up,
changed hands, was leveled off
to be a piece of some great parcel
that contracts call development.
It drifted probably, shifted gears
                    or merely stopped.

The forward march leaves behind
the frame for picture postcards.
How could the corporate heart
                be served
by flowers pressed in Camus' book
or lacy vintage valentine?

Someone said
the cafe turned into a cycle shop.
                    I don't know.
It does roll on inside imagination,
perfect to the crumpled napkin
coffee ill-attended getting cold
the waiter growing old before our eyes.
The unimportant conversations
                    were always more important
than warmness on the inside trickling down
                    black coffee might provide.
And anyway the warmness up ahead was coming
and it was always better, best.

Suspense would always stop by for a chat.
More than just a part of love,
suspense is head foreplay.

I see it clearly now,
each day that dynamited into night
as though it were this night ahead.

                    And you,
a vapor all around me, in me.
I always thought the larger part
of heaven, hell or here
was the ambiance we carried to it.

Your breath is ever on me
                    and a little damp.
Perhaps some San Francisco mist collected
                    through the decades
                    and distilled,
waits here to fall when I come back.

So this is purgatory.
The memory set in mold.
Reality a little way past reach.

I wait.
Tomorrow then, or soon
you'll reach and pull me up
                    and into heaven.

A bow has little competition
                with an untied ribbon.
And bud before a flower opens
stays on stem unnoticed.

You cannot praise a bloom
beyond the blossom seen effectively.
As Steinian as that may be and is,
it's also truth beyond all truths.
And our cafe, now vacant lot or worse,
is still and always Our Cafe,
waiting there for us to enter in
through hardly open, hard-to-open door.

A Letter Never Sent

Some nights your sighs
do not tear up the blackness
on other nights they boil it down
                          to nothing.
It comes and goes.
A quarrel over lovers,
a dare not taken up.
Love, a cup half full,
not filling up again.

By what divining light
does heat turn into mildew?
Where does the blurring start
between providence and progress?

Ever up ahead
            another river road.
Another blank page to be filled
and one more beating heart,
someone would like to stop,
            that won't be stilled.
And this is but another letter
that I never sent
            and never meant to.

Dostoyevsky Lived Here

Images compound.
You threading traffic,
head above the walkers
on a Monday winter day—
your stride and gait
as though in purpose,
when you were only strolling
          to be strolling.
I think of you in motion,
                    always.
Never languid on a couch with bonbons
or prisoner to television
          after supper and the dishes.
The dozens of you turn in every hour
afraid of what you'll miss
while not revolving.

I see you running,
eyes at constant blink.
The head inside the skull
          in narrow roll.
Brain ever working,
left to right, head to front,
          no cell celibate.
A smile always,
or some other decoration
that will not leave your face reposed.
Your arms go 'round me
and even then adjust.
                    Busy fingers.
Your hands at times at needlework.
Writing letters. Sorting papers.
                    Jigsaw puzzling.
Stroking Sybel, our first cat.
And at the window box
you water in a pattern
that the plants appreciate.

In a hurry always,
to and never from.
Ever tiptoe poised atop a ladder
at the topmost bookshelf
rummaging but little through the volumes
since they are stored and catalogued
                              in secret thought.
Your lips part not so much in conversation
                              or the yawn
but more in silent thinking.
Perception bubbles to the surface
but every sentence is commuted
before it finds its oral frame.

I see you. Often are you here
                    in steady glide.
You float and sift through afternoons
that hurry with you.
The two of you impatient for the night.

Motorlike, without the noise.
Ferris wheel, sans calliope.
Metronome. No clicks.
You are clockwork without time.
And yet nerve endings never show.
Your gait is more the music box
that needs no eye to be appreciated.

I watch afar at times
            and do not enter in.
But when I ride the carousel
I ride with you in sync.
Observer, I am only that—
no pressure to be up and in the circle
as you do Autumn acrobatics.

You somersault in Summer too.
No season and no hour favored.

Abed you take your ease alive.
Love does not pass between us
                  it comes shuffling.
Arms and legs and eyes converge.
Never, never hammer-like or slithering,
above the bed we sail
                  not caught in pillow.
We do not copulate, we flow as river,
no finish line or starting gate—
                  no end and not beginning.
I am a third
that sees the two of us at love
as if reporting to the city desk.
One mouth between us over there
                  how can we breathe?
Air flows in and out of us
            as fair as air is fair.

We are each other's wheel
and axle well aligned.

I know *one* is the common noun
          in lovers' conversation,
but looking on at distance
I see us onelike and no other way.

It all comes rushing to me in a rush
                              hill
                    the
              climb
          to
      begin
      I
As
these decades later.
Perfect, unembellished memory.

I'd lay at rest
what I dredge up each day
          if I were able.
I am not.
I go hiking Stanyan Street
          as if to crystal thought.

I must be seeking punishment.
There is no perfect peace or crime
while time is arbiter.

A child's balloon, bright red in color,
                    floats heavenward
until it's but a dot, then nothing.
Somewhere off beyond it's magnified,
                    becomes a globe.
So too the thought
that feeds upon itself grows larger, rarified.

Another Visit to the Hill House

Here in this now abandoned room
I see the tracings of you still
the memories not killed by polish,
old furniture exchanged for new.
You brush against me not as ghost
                          but as yourself.
That is a haunting true
and it will not be stilled
by looking at an unflocked wall.

The cobweb of that life that was
is fine rice paper turned to steel.
The memory of it nothing less
                          than what it is
truer every day.

I do not avoid, I welcome.

If I'd have been that fisherman,
etched in pencil. Painted in in blue.
The one that hung above the bed
intimidating with his perfect form,
I might have lasted, even been
what time imagines for a moment
then rejects before rejecting heart
from other self can enter in.
I might have stood on firmer ground
by that I mean a surer bed
and been that fisherman
              I wished I'd been.

The heart, the head is led, is made,
ever afterward and worse
to burst with hindsight.

If is the armor every lover
wears when dredging long ago.
It is the safety valve that keeps
the dump truck bed in quarter air
allowing only surface kindling
to tumble to already crowded ground.

God damn the fisherman in blue
that I held up as yardstick.
Some Dorian, somewhere
is melting fast
the looking glass shouts back an image
                    that was never there.
If not, there is no justice anywhere.

A Message to the Contractor Concerning Jorge Bolet's Reinvention of Rachmaninoff

Tear down the walls, but please
do not attack the grass.
Leave ivy to its own imagination
even as you pull the creeper from
                the eaves and side boards.

And as you stand and swing
                that newly sharpened scythe
cutting down our lives above the root
can you remember when our kisses came
                like information,
so new and so inventive we could only
wonder at the ones next coming,
marvel as they did and wonder on?

It was, I think, July.
(But love remembered
always seems to wear a summer dress.)
We had been to hear
Bolet invent Rachmaninoff,
the Third Concerto with its complicated thirds.
Words were springing from his fingers
falling on us like a blossom drift
and you were not so sleepy anymore.
I had died and gone to heaven
                in the second movement.
You went ahead at the cadenza.

You never met me but went on ahead,
your transport was the music same as mine
but different destinations are the dreamer's rule
not exception when Bolet is playing Liszt
            or that so difficult Sergei.

I beg you now to spare the grass.
Cart off the bricks and boards and clutter
            but leave the clover to the clover.
And leave us trembling still and trapped
inside the looking glass, Bolet as buddy.
I ask that you not muddy up
            that backyard place,
that slice of once green paradise
now going brown.

To forget is to ever chance remembering.

The City As Ocean

The hills rise up
like water walls,
waves in solid glacier.
Held in place
by pasted plankton
seen as grass,
gray asphalt rubbings;
as here and there
a rock breaks through
to further hinder
        navigation.

Fog lives,
is part of every hilltop
and hill bottom.
A soft Saran-wrap
        wraparound.

The little boats
that cables pull
sound bells as pure
as bobbing buoy
and as predictable.
And there's the lighthouse
                safe secure,
atop some masoned mansion
from preceding century.
Its beacon, window wide,
hard light is seen as far
as two hills over.

Great ships there are
that thread amid
the tied together boats.
They motor through
never float or coast
these measured waters.

The city seen
as wider ocean
is not thought,
or mean invention
made to make
a table top
for prose to play on.
Fact is the reason
seas must be surveyed
maps remade, redrawn.
What sailor knows
beyond the doubting
where seacoast ends
and land begins?

And where's the port?
                Not here.
Somewhere further inland.

If cautious captain
and depend-on crew
is not the soul
of seas and sailing,
where ticks the heart
of such a land-sea mass?
This body undulating,
              with itself,
self-congratulating,
ever kissing—
soft caressing, shoreline.
Evil in the argument
with lover wind
and good friend sky,
the sea as city
is twin-bodied
and at odds.

If there are gods
they gave the ocean
              soul.

No ocean rolls
without direction.
No river threads
without a needle eyelet
        hollowed out
to thread through.
If tides are booked
they have a course,
not merely cosmic,
or why the upset
when they misbehave
or don't perform
at scheduled time?
And here we come
to mind and thought.

Is it unthinkable
that some things
        unexplainable
remain just that?

All cities growing
from a shoreline
cannot be likened
to their neighbor,
larger, wider ocean—
singled out
with such security.
Only San Francisco.
We don't know why.

It has to do
with fluctuation,
not attitude
or even those
wall-water hills.

Added energy supposed,
attempted attitude perhaps.
No, not even that.

Ebb and flow.
Ebb and flow—
give and take
in other places
cause this town,
this round wet city,
to be sea-same.
Calm in sunlight,
cold and glittering.
          Dangerous
in dark of night
and frightening.
But always honest,
          ocean-like,
without apology.

Ask any sailor
which sea holds
the great adventure.
He will answer
San Francisco every time.

Comets

for Cliff Graubart

The line I like the best
is the one that goes
from here to there,
uninterrupted and without detour.

Two by Four

Here a graying scholar stands
and rails against the age arriving.
Youth, he says, is clumsy
unsuited, ill-prepared to take its place,
if such a place exists.

The manchild only tweaks the old man's beard
and questions, *were you ever young?*
Probably not, the old man grumbles,
                    probably not.

Fun at the Fair

for Aram Saroyan

The night's an attic
to the bedroom earth.
To know our worth we need
the hike upstairs
        and to the basement, too.
What comes and goes
on stairways, stairwells?
            Only life.
Those who will not take the time
to traverse, trip, trot on
will miss not just the eagle
but the eagle's song.

So swift a piece of life,
so slight a thing
we are today, tomorrow,
not what tomorrow brings.

The poet stumbles, gets up
runs to find his catch up time—
he is the *mystic warrior*
            in the underbrush.

The general dies a martyr,
and poet dies a pauper
and in-between the in-betweens
are led off to the slaughter.

All life is after life
and we are marking time,
while time, that rural enemy,
has marks on each of us
            (birth and brand).
The fortuneteller's lifeline
the gimmick drawn on every hand.

Ah, but there is fun
not merely melancholy
to be found at every fair
a hopscotch smear on city sidewalks,
a defrocked millionaire caught
with his pants down 'round his ankles.

The sanctity of Santa Clauses
invaded by the baron on the hill
amuses us until we need
St. Nicholas ourselves.

From the Observation Deck

The silence is crowing because the cock is silent.

A gaggle of philosophers gather at the corner
in unmarked cars. Later they will be arrested
for reconnoitering.

A Chesire cat with false moustache
and blinders on is directing traffic.

Greeks caught gifting bears with retsina
have been taken to an asylum in North Carolina.

Last week's politicians are still carrying boxes
of worn-out grudges. Goodwill Industries has refused
to accept them as a tax-free donation.

Several dogs are meowing and with good reason.

A television interviewer is inventing history by giving the shrubbery cue cards. He has interviewed a local Stop Sign and is setting up for Go. Yellow flashes and he becomes confused. He is fired for staging a crosswalk fight.

A mail-order bride has reached the dead letter office and is opening her wedding presents.

Hannibal is crossing an elephant with ice.
He hopes to get a highball that remembers.

The government of a capitalist country is being cheered by its people for doing good works.

(Which one of the preceding statements is false?)

Safety in Numbers

Such a little sin it was
      on such a giant day
I thought the wind might pick it up
            and run it off.
But evening's here and no wind still
the sin is now near shoulder-high,
too big to lose itself in seas
it needs another sin or so,
if only just for company.

Impossible Requests

I would like to be the shop steward
            in the Butterfly Union.

I want to be owned by nothing I own.
I want to own nothing.

I desire to meet God in this life
so that I might keep an open mind
                    for the next.

If you have any worn-out ideas
or ideologies I will put them with my own
and together we will seek out a new
and less expensive blacksmith.

The Best Embraces

for Helga Sandburg

Oh, daughter of unchristened
        father of us all
you do me honor and great damage
in writing poems of me to me.
Honor because time is of such value
and you take yours to look beyond
        my paragraphs to me.
Trouble because ethic, protestant,
threatens that such gifts
should be returned in ample helping.
And how does one match prose with prose?

The muse is shuttling between us
not stopping once at other people's doors.

As surely as the best embraces
are intended and indelible
          looked back upon,
so too our energy floats back
and back between us. Mixes.
Hurries in and out again.

If spring is not inconstant
it is like the butterfly it hatches
carrying the memory of old blossoms
                    into new
and we shoot straight up from the earth
and cling in envelope of mist
unhurried and unbridled by
ancestors who would have us be
their heritage, continued voice.

We are ourselves, you more than most
your father's daughter but in name
your talent with its own voice only
not borrowed from another,
                    invented out of you.

And me, ah me—
your husband down the ages,
                    centuries,
just now in Barney's shadow.

A Poem Is a Little Thing

A poem is a little thing
it only journeys from itself
to ask if it can be of help
and then it journeys home again.
A poem is a little thing
not mighty like the sword
it never, ever runs away
it only moves ahead, toward.

Brel Remembered

for France Brel

They burned the cities when you died
because without you goods meant nothing,
                    the populace less.
And in the smoke that swirled
                    from each ensuing fire
no ghosts beckoned and no spirits danced.
It was as if your manuscripts helped kindle
every upward-reaching flame. Your name
over and over again falling back as ashes only.
Such is immortality. You are immortal while you live,
mortal only at death's gateway.

For John Ashbery

Sucking the sherbets, crooning the tunes,
naming the names.
Always the whiteness
sheets and milk and Myadec
blushes are unwanted here.
And yet no dream is quite so solitary
that you, in leaky pail,
could not bring it from
                    the blindness
into internal light.

You always work.
without a net and yet
if you should stumble
your own words
          would catch you
same as they catch up to us.

Mostly at night you trap us
after the light has gone.

Annie Dillard

Run when the first stone sings.
Flee when the sun sets down
                in eastern sky
or rises westward.
And hide, hide when rivers run uphill.
Go away.
Your talents can be put to better use
                on farther hill.
Ah, but your first suggestion
                made all the difference here.
All the Tinker Creeks you spawned
                now flow together
in a different kind of river.

Charles Plymell Goes to Prison

I always knew
they'd get you, Charlie,
they've all been jealous
            of your gift.
Did you suppose that you could drift
through life poetically, unapprehended?
If so the odyssey has ended.
You've been marked man
since you were luncheon meat
'tween Burroughs' bread
            and Ginsberg Gulden—
Neal nosh on the side—
When North Beach was North Beach.

I'd go your bail
but that same lynch mob's
            after me.
I'll do what I can, Charlie.
There is a great kinship
            on this journey.
But don't buck, Charlie,
            don't buck.
Tenure's only tenure
You can't wish it into bread.
The rod that pushes you is permanent,
the one that strikes you's temporary.

In Search of Norman Mailer

Joe, I read your advert
on the shithouse wall
                    at Morro Bay.
I didn't write the number down
for I had nothing I could give
to one so desperate and needing.
But I thought you ought to know
that all of us who deal in words
are only writing advertisements
                        for ourselves.
You can be faulted only
                in your penmanship,
not for your penciled and outreaching cry.

I hope a dozen dozen ring you up
and bring Utopia to your first meetings.
Myself, I send the season's greetings.
Would it were myself.

I Was Thinking of Lillian Roxon

I was thinking today of Lillian Roxon
            I don't know why
maybe because there was too much seacoast
                  bubbling
or too many obvious Sunday fillers
            in too big a Sunday paper.

She was a wonder, she was,
all wide and Aussie and handsome and more.
She never stopped opening doors for me
            that others tried to close.

I don't suppose she's in heaven now, not her,
too hellbent and set in her ways
to get up for angels on Sunday morn
but oh, she could turn a phrase and be gone
                and she was.
Away to forever, she'll never be back.
Some Sundays are gray
when I think of my darlin' Lilli.
Today was just such a day as that,
it slid down the hill, bent over,
folded its arms and died.

Options

for Jane Campbell

There are other paradises
than those we're always promised,
        some easier to reach.
A plan thought out,
a well-laid table,
a borderline that's blurred
        and needs no sentries.

A well-made coat against the cold
is paradise enough for me this year.
I know that I'll want more
within the new age coming.
Each man's needs should far exceed
                            his grasp
or what are needs for?

I think that heaven now
would be some woman's arms.
Some woman I have yet to meet
and be tripped up by.
Tomorrow I might think the road's end
                        heavenly.

124

One ought to have an option
and yet be covered in the final hour.
Back then to scriptures
and the studying of same.
The one insurance policy
those of us who fear and love
our God in equal measures
dare not be found out without.

Vocational Training

Why no mermaids stopping here—
no sirens waving rock to rock.
Have beach dogs chased them off
to warmer, bluer seas?

I asked a river boy if he
might give directions or some clue
as to the whereabouts
            of even albatross.
He said *I only work here part time.*
That's the loss,
temporary, superseding full employment.
The ribbon cut so near the starting gate.

Christchurch to Duneden

for Lyn Gamwell

Sheep graze along the roadside
alone,
   in pairs,
      bunched like hedges
         or scattered
like the dandelion in the short grass.
Heads bent over nibbling at nothing
they balance like Wallendas
        on the tips of cliffs.
Drover gone, sheep dog absent
each ewe and lamb examines
           at its leisure
new grass, newer clover.

It is the perfect Saturday
to be moving down the highway
from Christchurch to Duneden
until a wide-winged eagle
picking at the carcass of a possum
is hit head-on by auto in high drive
                    ahead of us.

The eagle leaps and dances
for a moment on the hood,
an ornament awry,
then hits the windscreen in its death throes
spinning with an epileptic urgency,
bouncing to the ground. My eyes close.

I blink, wake up and turn the page
of one more letter
filled with no's disguised as yes
as if to question what I'm after.

What I wanted and I want
is your head head on,
            belly, belly up
in anteroom or acreage afar.

Oh heart, you are much quicker
than the eyelid flickering
but never, never fast enough.

Some kilometers gone
a wounded, dying eagle lies,
new tires punch it into pulp
no scavenger would bother with.
What troubles have I large enough
that I would dare to sort them out
            on this same road?

We'll meet in Wellington you say,
                but why?
I have not yet learned
some new way to say I stumbled.

Didn't you see me . . .
and would you have broken the fall?

Going Home: A Question of Balance

for Sam Crocker

Beretta's gone.
That voice so haunting
in the Porter/Coward song
          has not been stilled
but now fills other halls,
sends new lovers home
to fresh-made bed and breakfast
in Eastern cities.

Ginsberg comes home on occasion
and Snyder carries North Beach ever onward—
not so much a tattered banner
(the City Lights have never dimmed)
but now it's more a whim to him than cause.

Because the old haunts haunt us
          I go back.
And yes you can go home again—
sameness, once allowed to set
will supersede each change
and what we find and namecall strangeness.

Those of us addicted,
infected with dependency of time and place,
will always have a home here,
                if not homecoming.
What serves and saves us
is our own hard overriding need
forever pumping adrenaline into the landscape.

I arrive furloughlike
on R. & R. without the hell-raise bent
knowing no one anymore but knowing
                                there are those
convinced beyond mere reckoning
                that they know me.

It's true
you are not hero in your own hometown
unless you've got a weekly series running
                or rerunning every day.
But even that is danger-bent.
The mask must never slip.
The dancer must waltz endlessly,
he's not allowed to dip or turn
                or do-si-do, without rehearsal.

Still San Francisco always gives back
              better than we give.
It is a luxury to merely walk the wharf.
Day workers jingle take home pay
that would stagger millionaires,
coin of the realm in ambiance.
But none of us are heroes
                    in a hero city.
Praise singers only.

Caen's Baghdad or Dong Kingman's splashy thrust
are pastel backdrops for the Ferlinghetti muse,
                    mad or merry.
Every Delaplane postcard home
              is not greeted with surprise
and Pike went mad at sunrise.

O'Flaherty will talk convincingly
              of how the old town's gone,
Keene eyes no longer look from every gallery,
(ample argument for plus and minus still).
Sparky's strip's been quartered,
                    cut apart,
analyzed more often than Miss Doda's.
He survives, we all do.

It is the city and surrounding squares
                    that give us give and take.
Adversaries each and wide.
Being in and out of one another's favor
                    and embrace
cause each of us to try the longer stride
                                    next time.

José, that Sunday diva with soprano reach
                    should set it all to music.
Butterfly in one act only.

Can you imagine Ginsberg
not yet declared a monument by government?
It's tantamount to winking off Niagara
and Grand Rapids in a single blink or wank.
So he comes home to San Francisco,
                    now and then.
Lots of give and take here, not just take.

When I was younger, way back when,
Willie Kapell slam-dashed into
                    a San Francisco mountain top.
No one's made a painting
                    or a poem of it yet.
(Not even one of eighteen variations.)

Most San Francisco tragedies stay unadorned.
This lack of advertisement
                is what makes The City great.

True, the *Chronicle* chronicles
each leap from bridge, keeps count.
But names of divers are not etched on pilings.
Death is not always dignified by chisel
as life is not propelled by good words only.
Oh, but we love the adjectives
                and we should do so
                        while we can.
They are the perfect lovers every time.
And when they change
to fast friends or to worse
they needn't cause an early death
                or banishment.
It's only time to go away again.
This is the city that remembers to forget.
Wassermann tests have gone the way of rabbits,
truth has a good name bay to bay.

Have I been too gentle with the neighborhood,
                              perhaps.
But there'll be letters, sub-headlines—
that will tell me if I went too far
                    or did not venture far enough.
Never gossip, though. (Perhaps a whisper in Marin.)
It's too fragmented up here for all that
and it's the fragments come together
that have made the rock
on which to build the home
                    for visitation.

Beretta's gone, but she'll be back.
Meanwhile the lovers each make private plans
for bed and breakfast and attack.
And those of us who travel
                    from the city
know the best credential
we can trot out in fast company
is news of where we came from.

Hope

Over our shoulders always
but always up ahead.
The grin that moves to laughter
the smile that moves to word
the thought that moves to doing
                      something good.
The promise is the promise.
We seldom have to hunt it down.
It finds us by its own direction.

Nebraska Sonnets

for Bruce Bowden

This land is not as flat
       as it pretends to be
but wider than it says it is.
And deep, deep.

I Woods in the Leaving

The moment comes when woods go off
Fast falling like the final leaf
A murmur in their tops, a cough
Then disappearing fast. The thief
Who comes and cautious enters in
Is so much like the woods and they
Are bandits too as each attends
And woos us, then it's swift away.

Birch are strolling down the hill
Elms run to meet them in their stride
A maple's at the gate, see how
The willow's arms are open wide.
Come here, he whispers, hurry now,
We'll march and stay together till . . .

II A Shifting

What is it that the winter wind has warned?
A blizzard's pushing that oncoming breeze
With all the might of wizard 'buked and scorned.
It tops the very tops of ancient trees.
And yet the snow is innocence
As white gives way to whiter shade.
If ice can yet make semblance and sense
It dies in river childbirth. Spring's repaid.

The grass advances and the snow recedes.
Is it some measure of humanity
That God attends to all our earthly needs?
Or merely His own kind of vanity
That He's perceived as doer of good deeds?
Whatever. There is no use in anarchy.

III Evensong

If love were all I had to give
I'd give it and be done.
There are no others anywhere, not one.
It is for your own breath I live
God gives me no alternative
And I have looked not left or right
Since sighting you within my sight.
You are for me the only time imperative.

Oh, let me be the one who lies
Against your side for always and
Inside your size, inside your sighs
To do whatever you command,
And see but what you'd have me see.
I am your bread, partake of me.

IV Country Gardens

These fields were meant to plow and plan
By muscled voices raised in song.
The dignity of farm and farming man
Is not a crookstick or the devil's tong
But solid, bold and easy to define.
Earth honey from land honeycomb,
Long furrows planted line on line.
A play space for God's lesser works to roam.

The field mouse tunneling in far banks,
The cat in conquest sitting in the road,
The weasel, ears up, eyes closed, giving thanks,
He's finally found diversified abode.
All creatures as opposed to all mankind
Know farmers are the nearest God they'll find.

V Clouds

Let us address the clouds again
Those soft gray-tinged unbleeding things
That cause the heart its wonderings.
They are the food of let's pretend.
Fleece too good for best of men.
Their misty mountain offerings
Are saved, I think, to give to kings.
Still let us to them now attend.

Oh clouds, in your pale morning gowns
Tramped down by angel feet and spur
To tell of your unending rounds
Would cause the speech to stop or slur.
You bump and float and blunder by
As if there were no under sky.

VI Preventive Medicine

Houses die, the same as men
They wither, shrivel and fall down.
Only the ground is neutral then
As houses are hacked and trucked to town.
The bigger the building, the stronger the axe,
The swifter the blow that fells.
I don't know how a house can relax
Whenever its owner sells.

Quick, caulk the basement, a leak has sprung
And there by the chimney a crack
A hole where a picture once was hung
Needs a new coat of shellac.
This dwelling place we hold so dear
Should see its doctor twice a year.

VII Anger Amplified to Sorrow

I had five sons, they did me well
Went off to school and off to war.
Four came home, a truth I tell
I loved the one who stayed the more.
Oh, he was cocky and a man
Not like his brothers, weak and small.
Bill drove the tractor down the land
Before he learned to climb the wall.

Peter comes to see me now
And Teddy too and Paul and Tom
They take a turn at turning plow
With steady hand and eager arm.
I'm not ashamed to say it still
I'd trade the four away for Bill.

VIII The River Platte

Between calm and calamity
She runs, she crawls, she flows
As if to reach her end is all she knows.
As soft as her serenity
Divine is her divinity.
She can't be trusted when she grows
Too big for her midwinter clothes
And hostages humanity.

I always thought a river should
Be like a lifeline in a way.
Not always altogether good
But not so much the other way.
The Platte, she's not like Robin Hood,
What she brings in she takes away.

IX The Knowing

The barn's well stored and we can sleep
It's been an early harvest home.
The cellar's stocked with apples steep
In preparation for the still unknown.
The fruits have bubbled on the stove and now
They're paraffined and sealed in Kerrs.
Before the fire we dwell on how,
Every if, and all the never weres.

There's something I have not yet said
It hangs between us like a little death
Some nights when we lie in the bed
We seem to hide inside each other's breath.
It's then I feel that you know too,
You took the wrong road, didn't you?

Index of First Lines

About the Author

Rod McKuen was born in Oakland, California, in 1933. At eleven, he left home to work and help support his family with odd jobs that took him throughout the western United States as rodman on a surveying unit, cowhand, lumberjack, ditchdigger, railroad worker, and finally rodeo cowboy. His first attention as a poet came in the early fifties, when he read with Kerouac and Ginsberg at San Francisco's Jazz Cellar. After serving two years as an infantryman in Korea, he returned as a singer of folksongs at San Francisco's Purple Onion. Before becoming a best-selling author in the 1960s, McKuen had been a contract player at Universal Studios and a vocalist with Lionel Hampton's band and had amassed a considerable following as a recording artist and nightclub performer.

His books, numbering more than forty titles, have been translated into some thirty languages and make him the best-selling, most widely read poet of his time. His film music has twice been nominated for Academy Awards (*The Prime of Miss Jean Brodie* and *A Boy Named Charlie Brown*). His classical works—symphonies, concertos, suites, and song cycles—are performed by leading orchestras and artists throughout the world. *The City: A Suite for Narrator & Orchestra*, commissioned by the Louisville Orchestra, was nominated for the Pulitzer Prize in Music.

He has written songs for nearly every important performer in the music business, producing standards that include "If You Go Away," "Seasons in the Sun" (both written with French composer Jacques Brel), "Love's Been Good to Me," "Jean," "I Think of You," "The World I Used to Know," "Rock Gently," and "I'll Catch the Sun." Those compositions, among others, have earned the writer-composer-performer more than forty gold and platinum records worldwide. He is considered one of the few major performers who can guarantee "sold out" concerts throughout the world.

Despite his many ongoing careers, writing occupies most of his time. Rod McKuen poetry is currently taught in schools, colleges, universities, and seminaries around the world. He is recipient of the Carl Sandburg and Walt Whitman Awards for outstanding achievement in poetry and the Brandeis University Literary Trust Award for "continuing excellence and contributions to contemporary poetry." With over forty million books of poetry in print, the author has no intention of resting on his laurels. He still writes "every day of my life" on the road, in the rambling California Spanish house he shares with his animals, or in his part-time "digs" in Australia.

He is currently finishing a new musical composition for full symphony orchestra which will have a dual premiere in Paris and London next year.